DONE DEAL

YOUR GUIDE TO MERGER AND ACQUISITION INTEGRATION

M. Beth Page

Published by *Authenticity Press*

Editing: Phyllis Kennelly and Pam Withers
Cover design and inside page layout: Dale Costanzo
Proofreading: Sharon McInnis

Printed and bound in Canada

Authenticity Press address: *www.authenticitypress.com*

Library and Archives Canada Cataloguing in Publication

Page, M. Beth, 1964-
    Done deal : your guide to merger and acquisition integration / M. Beth Page ; editors, Phyllis Kennelly and Pam Withers.

Includes bibliographical references.
ISBN 0-9739130-1-0

    1. Consolidation and merger of corporations. 2. Personnel management. I. Withers, Pam II. Kennelly, Phyllis III. Title.

HD2746.5.P33 2005   658.3   C2005-906142-1

Dedication

This book is dedicated to my parents,
Barbara and Carl Page.
Thank you for your love and support.

About the Author

Beth Page provides organization development consulting and coaching services in collaboration with her clients. She has managed organization development and human resources in a variety of roles for over 10 years.

Beth has a Master of Science in Organization Development from Pepperdine University, and a Master of Science in College Student Personnel from Western Illinois University. She has also completed the Advanced Human Resources Management program at the University of Toronto, the Certificate in Management Development from the School of Business at Carleton University, and a Bachelor of Arts in Psychology at Carleton University.

Beth is the owner of Dream Catcher Consulting, a firm dedicated to working with organizations to integrate the human dimension with business results.

Acknowledgments

I am grateful to many people who supported this project both directly and indirectly. Thank you for your support.

I had an expert panel of researchers, authors and consultants who provided invaluable input and feedback on my research. They included: Ron N. Ashkenas, Anthony F. Buono, Richard M. DiGeorgio, Timothy J. Galpin, David B. Jemison, Jeffrey A. Krug, Mitchell Lee Marks, and Nick J. Mastracchio Jr. Internal practitioners at Best Practice companies at HP, Cisco, GE Capital and Johnson & Johnson participated in interviews to review the best practices results and to offer the internal M&A practitioner's perspective.

The original nudge came from Judith Gibson who encouraged me to write this book. I am also grateful to Phyllis Kennelly. She is the first person who read my book and helped bring order and clarity to my message.

I am indebted to Laura Min Jackson for her friendship, support, and the valuable assistance I received from her on the 5C planning Worksheets. I was fortunate to have Barbara Harrison review and comment on early drafts of the book. Clare Mann and Dawn Brown are two dear friends and authors who always had words of wisdom and encouragement for me. Louise McDonald, Doris Kiiffner, Jim Flood, Sheila Flood, Susan Atkinson, Lynda Penderly and Leslie Smith offered their friendship and support throughout the project.

I have the Canadian Association of Professional Speakers to thank for introducing me to Stephen Hammond and Ronald Coleman, two authors who offered referrals, encouragement, and guidance as the book reached the final stages. Thanks to their generosity, I was referred to Pam Withers, who provided the final editing and Dale Costanzo, who completed the cover art and inside page layout. Sharon McInnis provided final proofreading. I benefited from the professional support of Keijo Isomaa of Morriss Printing to meet the final printing deadline. I am grateful to each of you for your professionalism, your wonderful sense of timing and enthusiasm for the book.

To the many friends and family members who believed in me, thank you for cheering me on.

Notice to Readers

The information in this book is offered as an aid to developing and maintaining professional competence, with the understanding that the author and publisher are not providing legal or other professional advice.

Exercise your professional judgment about the correctness and applicability of the material.

The author, publisher and vendor make no warranties or representation regarding the outcome or the use to which the information in this book is put and are not assuming any liability for any claims, losses, or damages arising out of the use of this book.

Table of Contents

Preface

Done Deal is written for you if you have been dissatisfied with the outcomes of previous Merger and Acquisition (M&A) involvement or if you are about to participate in your first M&A.

A M&A is a significant change management activity involving employees, shareholders, business units, customers, and many other stakeholders. Recognizing the human dimension of M&A integration is vital. Employees often feel like M&As are done to them. They feel powerless, out of control and betrayed by a process that results in significant changes, particularly for employees at acquired companies. The M&A team must address the issues and concerns of the whole system.

The *5C Integration Model*™ is a change management model that resulted from my research as a professional Organization Development practitioner. The model is designed to offer professionals a different way of approaching M&A activity. Incorporating the *5Cs* and the best practices identified by experts in the field will deepen your understanding of the M&A process. The model will also allow you to anticipate the impact of M&A on the human dimension and execute activities that will increase the potential for M&A to be a collaborative partnership with everyone involved.

Introduction

When are mergers and acquisitions a *Done Deal*? It depends on who you ask. Shareholders regard the deal as done when shareholder value increases. CEOs will say it's when the acquired company's products start shipping under a single label. Employees, who pay close attention to promises made to them during a merger and acquisition, might say the deal is never done.

Done Deal takes the view that the merger and acquisition is complete when the integration of the two companies is complete, not when the deal is announced to the marketplace or consummated according to a legal or financial transaction.

Mergers and acquisitions (M&As) are a significant activity for many organizations. Yet most mergers are not successful, primarily because the "merger of two organizations is actually a merger of individuals and groups," according to Buono and Bowditch, authors of *The Human Side of Mergers and Acquisitions: Managing Collisions Between People, Cultures, and Organizations.*

A merger means that two previously separate organizations are combined into a third, new entity. An acquisition involves the purchase of one organization for incorporation into the new parent firm.

Unfortunately, few M&As involve an effort to integrate different cultures and workforces, even though M&A activities bring about significant change involving employees, organizational entities, systems, shareholders, customers, and many other stakeholders.

Companies initiate M&As for numerous business objectives, ranging from achieving market entry to gaining proprietary technology. Companies that want to expand strive to acquire businesses that enhance their product portfolio and secure additional employees with specialized skills. But too many enter into M&A activity without recognizing the impact on the organization and the overall affect on the human element within the two merging companies. M&A activities that do not meet corporate objectives can result in lost revenue, customer dissatisfaction, and employee attrition issues.

M&A researchers, consultants, and internal practitioners agree that using transition teams, an integration manager, and a comprehensive employee communications strategy rank among the best practices. They help increase the success of merger and acquisition activity.

Done Deal features the original research I conducted with a key group of internal and external M&A experts. They generously shared their knowledge and enabled me to develop a summary of best M&A practices. *Done Deal* also features the *5C Integration Model*™, a unique paradigm I created after completing my research and conducting an extensive review of M&A academic and business literature. The *5C Integration Model*™ encompasses communication, courtship, cultural compatibility, confidentiality, and completion. It provides useful and thought-compelling keys designed to strengthen the chances of successful merger and acquisition integration.

1

The Case for Strengthening M&A Integration

M&As represent a significant expense for corporations worldwide. Thirty thousand M&As took place in the United States by 1998, at a cost of $1.5 trillion (Marks & Mirvis, 1998). Worldwide M&As totalled $2.4 trillion that same year. And the costs keep increasing. JP Morgan reported that firms spent $3.3 trillion on M&A activity in 1999, up 32% from the previous year.

Corporations use M&As to realize organizational synergies not attainable by each company operating autonomously. They also pursue M&As to achieve market entry, establish brand image, gain access to strong distribution channels, gain proprietary technology, cut costs, and achieve efficiencies. Another M&A business objective is to grow globally. Finally, some companies decide to purchase others because they believe it's easier to achieve certain objectives through acquisition than through internal development, particularly in time-sensitive market environments.

Increasing the Success and Value of M&As

The volume of M&A activity is increasing despite documented reports that shareholders, particularly in the acquiring company, are not realizing value.

In fact, more than three-quarters of corporate combinations fail to attain projected business results. Most produce higher-than-expected costs and lower-than-acceptable returns, according to Marks and Mirvis in their 1998 book, *Joining Forces: Making One Plus One Equal Three in Mergers, Acquisitions, and Alliances.*

Worse, academic literature documents a clear absence of best practices research to strengthen the success rates (DiGeorgio, 2002). Because many firms do not engage in M&A activity regularly, they have not developed a repeatable process. Even those with M&A experience often fail to learn from their successes and failures.

I've documented the factors that most commonly contribute to a poor M&A success rate, in Table 1.

Table 1: Common Factors Contributing to Poor M&A Success Rates
• Lack of business strategy for M&As
• Overpaying for the target firm
• Lack of due diligence
• Poor or nonexistent post-acquisition integration
• A desire to distract attention from the core business concerns
• Lack of a disciplined approach to the pre-acquisition process
• Conflicts within corporate cultures
• The M&A being treated as an engineering exercise
• Restructuring and downsizing activities that adversely impact the target company's productivity
• The lack of a systems approach to acquisitions

Also, as merger momentum mounts, organizations benefit from evaluating a M&A strategy against a list of potential showstoppers, provided by Marks and Mirvis, and highlighted in Table 2. Potential showstoppers can lead to a withdrawal from the deal. Other alternatives to withdrawing from the deal include changing the valuation of the acquisition or allocating more resources to manage the fallout.

Table 2: List of Potential M&A Showstoppers

- Distrust and incompatibility between managements
- Difficulties in working out governance arrangements
- Lack of talent to manage both ongoing operations and the transition
- Significant coordination costs required to obtain synergies
- Disruptions associated with the combination
- Threats to customer relationships as a result of the combination of two entities
- Incompatible values and culture
- Post-combination talent drain
- Impact on the workforce and communities

Best Company Practices

Rovit and Lemire studied 724 United States companies that together conducted 7,475 acquisitions between 1986 and 2001. From these, the researchers ultimately identified 110 firms that qualified as "frequent buyers." The study found that these frequent buyers created shareholder value, achieved returns above their cost of equity, and demonstrated the following series of common disciplines:

- started with small deals, institutionalized processes, and created feedback systems to ensure that buyers learned from their mistakes
- continually reviewed potential target companies, and kept ready lists of companies
- bought if the price was right
- built a standing team for deal making that participated in all acquisitions
- got line management involved early in due diligence
- devised clear guidelines for integration of acquisitions.

Even though these are the best practices, they are not implemented regularly. As a result, mergers are complex and rife with risk. Why? Because, as Buono and Bowditch confirmed in 1989, mergers demand more cooperation and interaction between partners than do acquisitions, where one firm takes over another. Most of the time, companies are looking for synergy, defined as competing better than anyone expected. Synergy yields a competitive advantage—efficiencies beyond what other market competitors require to survive. This leads indirectly to a practice known as "value capture," where redundant functions are eliminated to achieve financial benefit.

Achieving a *Done Deal*: Focusing on Integration

Several models exist for guiding a company through the M&A process, including Marks and Mirvis (1998), Buono & Bowditch (1989), and Galpin and Herndon (2000). *Done Deal* aims to focus practitioners on strengthening the integration process.

Companies that engage in frequent acquisitions tend to assume that post-merger integration eventually becomes a core competence. But integration efforts do not necessarily improve through repetition. Even companies with experience in this area fail to achieve both integration objectives and returns. Why? Because they neglect to set up mechanisms designed to review the process—mechanisms that lead to learning and future improvements.

Too often, firms focus on pre-announcement activities more than they do on integration itself. For example, since external advisors are typically rewarded for each completed transaction, they're far more motivated to complete the deal than to ensure that things run smoothly in the organization after they leave the premises.

Five Strategies for Strengthening M&A Results

Practitioners looking to strengthen M&A success need a variety of tools. One best practice entails approaching M&A as a change effort. Researchers have identified the following key activities:

- early integration planning of the organization, people, processes, and systems
- appointing an integration manager to oversee the integration process
- developing successful cultural integration strategies
- appropriately involving leadership during M&A activity.

The following five strategies can also strengthen M&A results:

1. Create an integration plan. Integration planning should be linked with due diligence and integration activities; the acquiring firm should use the time between the announcement and the closure to advance the integration planning. Wise use of this time can facilitate the decision-making process and help avoid "post-merger drift."

2. Appoint a strong integration manager and dedicate full-time staff to M&A activity.

3. Assess culture as part of due diligence. This assessment should be made before the deal is finalized, to avoid culture clashes that diminish the potential of the deal. The traditional M&A approach has included financial and legal evaluations of the acquisition target with little attention paid to the people and culture. Successful M&A strategies acknowledge and honor the importance of organizational culture as a critical element in the long-term integration success.

4. Have strong leadership in place to lead the integration effort. Organizational members will take their cues from the leadership responsible for the integration effort. Implement strong communication skills, an unwavering commitment to the integration, an openness with employees, and visible movement towards integration milestones and 100-day goals.

5. Attend to the human dimension that is part of all M&A activity. One of the most important resources a target organization has is its talent pool, yet the human dimension receives woefully inadequate attention during M&As. Fail to pay attention to the human dimensions and human dynamics of M&A activity, and you'll lose key talent. Organizations typically focus

on a target's intellectual property and capital, while failing to recognize the capabilities and strengths of their employees, even though the latter enhance their competitive edge. As researchers Pfeffer and Tromley put it, "see the workforce as a source of strategic advantage, not just as a cost to be minimized or avoided."

What human dimensions should firms involved in M&As explore? The employee's M&A experience, organizational restructuring and retention issues, and resistance to change.

2

M&A Integration Tools

M&A integration examines all the tasks and plans required to successfully bring the two companies together. Integration involves planning and implementing the new organization's processes, people, technology, and systems. It also entails implementing the consolidation, merging the cultures, and achieving the goals.

Although integration efforts traditionally focus on the organization's formal systems and processes, its informal systems and processes also require cultural integration.

Critical factors to consider during this stage are:

- the speed of integration
- the level of disruption staff and customers will experience
- communication with internal and external stakeholders
- many other issues unique to each integration activity.

Integration Planning

Unfortunately, because M&A practitioners often fail to link integration with pre-combination activities such as due diligence, they neglect questions of organizational fit in the early stages of acquisition analysis.

> *When the management of a company decides to merge with or acquire another company, it checks the financial strength, market position, management strength, and other health indicators of the other company. Rarely checked, however, are the "cultural" aspects: the company's philosophy or style, its technological origins which might provide clues to its basic assumptions, and its beliefs about its mission and future.* (Schein, 1997, pp. 268–269)

The greatest barrier to successful integration is cultural incompatibility. According to Edgar Schein, "the poor performance of many mergers, acquisitions, and joint ventures can often be explained by the failure to understand the depth of cultural misunderstanding that may be present." Research on cultural factors is the least likely to be undertaken as part of due diligence.

Integration planning, which takes cultural factors into account, should coincide with the initiation of due diligence. When these two are strongly linked, new corporate knowledge can facilitate consolidation.

When an intended M&A transaction is announced, employees of both companies expect change. The early days following the deal's close are a critical time for the company to initiate integration of the organization, processes, people, and systems.

Because the success of M&A activity is also influenced by the personal involvement of the individual facilitating the integration, his or her involvement should begin as early as possible. While due diligence and integration teams are often two separate entities, having them work in tandem rather than sequentially ensures that each team is getting the necessary data in the most timely and efficient manner.

Various integration options exist along a continuum, including operating as a separate holding company, having strategic control, operating as a managed subsidiary, having operational control, and finally operating as a merged and consolidated entity. M&A managers can evaluate and make critical decisions prior to negotiation if the initial decision on integration is not an option. What determines the degree of integration? The level of financial and operational synergies that the M&A activity can yield. Partial integration is an option if an acquirer wants to extend its market capability but maintain some of the operational strengths of the target firm.

Clean Teams

With the exception of regulatory and anti-trust concerns, integration planning can continue during the period between the announcement and the closing of the deal. One key mechanism is the creation of "clean teams," composed of experts who sign confidentiality agreements and who are assigned to play roles on various integration planning teams. The use of clean teams as part of the integration planning process allows companies to implement post-acquisition plans more quickly, especially since they are likely to make significant progress on integration planning during the period prior to the acquisition's completion.

The Integration Manager's Critical Role

An integration manager is responsible for overseeing the successful integration of all administrative, physical, organizational, and cultural aspects of the target company into the acquiring company. No wonder the role is widely viewed as one of the keys to M&A success! Up until the 1990s, the integration manager typically held a full-time role elsewhere in the organization, but over the past decade, this role has evolved to become designated as full-time on its own. That move followed the success of such companies as GE, whose Capital division pioneered the use of a full-time integration manager (an HR executive who had participated in the due diligence process). GE Capital asked that individual to serve as a guide to the new culture and to act as a bridge between Gelco, the company being acquired, and GE Capital.

Today, integration managers manage the integration process with an eye on the various challenges associated with cultural integration.

Exploring Cultural Integration

According to academic and business thought-leader John Kotter, "the biggest chore associated with an acquisition of any size is to merge the two (or perhaps more) different cultures. If this part of the transformation is ignored or handled poorly, problems will surface for years, maybe decades."

The importance of an organization's culture, particularly as a risk factor in M&A integration, cannot be underestimated. Harvard researchers report that firms that managed their culture realized a nearly seven-fold increase in revenue, compared with only 166% for firms that did not manage culture.

Yet specific, focused efforts to integrate different cultures and workforces remain the exception rather than the norm in M&A activity, and poor cultural compatibility continues to be cited as a factor in M&A failure. Cultural signs of the so-called "merger syndrome" include a "we versus they relationship, with a natural tendency for people to exaggerate the differences rather than the similarities between the two companies." (Marks & Mirvis, 1998)

Clearly, selecting a culturally appropriate model of integration is key to a successful *Done Deal*.

An organization's culture consists of the underlying values, beliefs, and principles that define an organization's management system, as well as the firm's management practices and behaviors that reinforce those principles. (Denison, 1990)

A more detailed definition of organizational culture comes from Dr. Edgar Schein, who defines it as the pattern of basic assumptions a given group has invented, discovered, or developed while learning to cope with external adaptation and internal integration challenges. The assumptions, says Schein, should "be taught to new members as the correct way to perceive, think, and feel in relation to those problems."

Keys for Successful Cultural Integration

Successful cultural integration begins with an early understanding of the cultural differences and processes that exist between the acquiring and target companies. Stages of culture clash include employees re-evaluating the way they do things, followed by viewing their way of doing things as superior to the other company. This is followed by attacking the other employees' way of doing things while defending their own. For a successful cultural integration to occur, each company should be coached to look at how the practices of the other company might be beneficial in the new entity. Conducting cultural due diligence early in the M&A due diligence process helps prepare the integration team as well as the companies' leadership for the efforts that are required to join together two distinct organizations.

Four-Step Approach to Cultural Due Diligence

Researchers have identified the following steps for conducting cultural due diligence:

1. Integrate cultural criteria early in the merger discussions.
2. Prepare due diligence teams with cultural criteria.
3. Have the due diligence teams collect data on culture.
4. Use tools to assess potential culture fit and issues.

How companies choose to deploy this model depends on their own structure and culture. Acquirers are encouraged to operate under the assumption that cultural differences exist, and they must actively work to manage these differences throughout the integration process. Companies are also encouraged to create joint projects that allow the teams to build success together. One large telecom company that actively engaged in M&A activity tasked one of its HR professionals with strengthening the company's acquisition process by educating executives and due diligence teams on culture.

Leadership During Change and Integration

Kotter defines "leadership" as coping with change. "The problem for us today," he adds, "is that stability is no longer the norm. And most experts agree that over the next few decades the business environment will become only more volatile."

Leadership becomes ever more critical as the pace of change in industry increases; Buono and Nurick have coined the metaphor of being in "permanent whitewater" to describe modern organizations, particularly those involved in M&A activity.

In the telecom industry, Unisys Chairman W. Michael Blumenthal provided a progressive example of leadership when he announced during one planned acquisition that the Burroughs and Sperry sales forces would be strengthened as part of the new organization. M&A researchers Mirvis and Marks note that Blumenthal's remark acted as a pre-emptive statement to the sales force to reduce potential attrition issues within the sales team, and signaled the company's commitment to maintain the two product lines—thereby providing reassurance to the customers, vendors, and employees.

Kotter's leadership model for leading large-scale organizational change includes the following eight-stage process:

- establish a sense of urgency
- create the guiding coalition
- develop a vision and strategy
- communicate the change vision
- empower employees for broad-based action
- generate short-term wins
- consolidate gains and produce more change
- anchor new approaches in the culture.

3

Focusing on the
Human Dimension of M&A

M&A activity is characterized in the academic literature as an "organizational marriage," complete with courtship. Cultural integration is often linked to a metaphor of a family where a parent who has departed is replaced by a step-parent. These relationship and familial metaphors illustrate the significant impact M&A activity can have on organizational life and its members.

M&As emerge from a managerial approach that values process, structure, formal roles, and indirect communication over people, ideas, and feelings. (Buono & Nurick, 1992).

Despite the importance of successfully integrating an organization's people and culture into a new entity, the published literature is filled with reports pointing to limited involvement from HR professionals in the early stages. This restricted involvement, in turn, limits HR professionals' ability to effectively influence the process. Unfortunately, legal and financial issues are given precedence over the possible traumas that might be experienced by organizational members impacted by M&A activity.

Employee Experiences

Organizational members undergoing an M&A can experience stress, anger, betrayal, frustration, and confusion. Some employees react by becoming preoccupied with their own self interests, such as their role in the new organization or job security. If they exhibit highly defensive and stressful behaviors, it is known as "merger syndrome."

Employees from a target company need to grieve the loss of the organization they have known before they can move forward with the change. Or, as Buono and Bowditch state, "merger-related organizational restructurings can traumatize and alienate people at all organizational levels."

Organizational Restructuring and Retention Issues

Layoffs, sometimes more ominously known as "value capture," "right-sizing," or "reductions in force," are too often one of the first activities after a M&A has been announced. Improperly handled, they will negatively impact retention among those who remain with the new organization.

Layoffs and turnover can and do happen at all levels of an organization. Approximately 25% of executives in acquired companies leave within the first year—a rate three times higher than companies not acquired. That's according to M&A researcher Jeffrey Krug, who reviewed business literature going back two decades to calculate that statistic. Another study shows that nearly one-half of senior managers in an acquired firm leave within one year, and 72% are gone within the first three years if retention efforts have not been made. (Tetenbaum, 1999).

To minimize departure rates, consider using alternative practices. Cisco, for example, had a "no layoff rule" as part of its acquisitions. When Wells Fargo made a particular acquisition, the firm undertook no reductions after an analysis of annual attrition rates suggested that recruitment would be required within six months of completing the acquisition.

Dealing with Resistance to Change

What of employees' resistance to change? Successful M&A practitioners know it's critical to identify and deal with it.

Organization consultant Kurt Lewin, who created an organizational change model, says pre-M&A attitudes, values, and behavior need to be "unfrozen" before an organization can successfully implement desired changes, then "refreeze" them at a new state.

It's vital to lay some groundwork for change to avoid employee resistance. People resist change for several reasons, including parochial self-interest, misunderstanding or lack of trust, different assessments, and low tolerance for change.

How can you help prepare an organization for change? Two options include polling and surveying the employee population, and developing information and communication strategies aimed at introducing opportunities for employees to participate in the change process.

M&A practitioners who respond to questions and concerns about structural, cultural, and role-related issues, and revise expectations, will achieve a degree of organizational stability.

Firms that engage in frequent M&A activity such as GE Capital, and Cisco use a systems approach that enables them to learn from experience, and make M&A activity a key business strength and competency.

One of the best practices employed by these companies is a learning mechanism designed to measure the factors contributing to M&A success and failure. In the spirit of continual learning and improvement, these firms document results from these assessments, then put resulting recommendations into practice.

4

The Experts Speak:
The Nine Best M&A Practices

In an attempt to identify the best M&A practices, prominent M&A researchers, consultants, authors and internal M&A practitioners whose companies were actively involved in M&A activity joined forces to conduct primary research. Nine best practices emerged from this work, which are followed by recommended action steps for applying these best practices.

1. Develop an Overall Strategy and Goal

Companies must establish long-range goals and objectives that consider future growth and how to attain it. They can establish a defined area of growth if M&A activities are compatible with these goals, and M&As represent a realistic means to meet the goal.

Internal M&A practitioners involved in the research were very clear on the corporate strategy behind their M&A activity. The M&A levers for the courtship range from expanding market share to acquiring technology or broadening the customer base.

Action Steps:

- Evaluate if the proposed M&A is consistent with corporate strategy.
- Conduct benchmarking to use as a guide to measure M&A progress.
- Be clear on the reasons the deal is being pursued.

---

2. Conduct Thorough Strategic, Financial, and Operational Due Diligence

Thorough examination of the target company is critical, particularly to assess strategic, operational, and financial elements before the deal is closed.

Strategic Due Diligence: Conduct comprehensive strategic due diligence assessments, including stakeholder analysis. Examine the key strategic levers associated with the merger and acquisition—ranging from human resources capabilities to sales and marketing strengths and weaknesses, cultural orientations, supplier networks and commitments. The key is to focus on those aspects of the M&A that are linked with the strategic intent of the combination.

Operational Due Diligence: Establish criteria that reflect the level of performance, the type of growth an individual company has, and the manner in which the company operates. Once a candidate company is identified, perform an extensive examination to see if the company is likely to meet expectations.

Financial Due Diligence: Develop a comparative financial profile of the two firms and retain the relative experts on valuation to value the target firm. If it is a merger, value both firms in order to measure the financial value and establish the relative ownership after the merger.

One internal practitioner suggested that the acquiring company for the M&A target must consider the opportunity to build value for its firm. Another internal M&A practitioner articulated the need to answer the question, "Why are you doing the deal?". Everyone considered communication vital throughout the courtship.

Experts assessed the strategic, financial, and operational due diligence best practices as interlinked. Where there is respect for confidentiality during the courtship phase, the investigation of the target company will be more productive. Next, M&A experts made initial assessments to help companies understand how the products fit into the corporate portfolio, to assess the talent at the target company, to evaluate its capabilities and risk of attrition, to assess the financial health of the target organization, to assess the operational capability of the organization to deliver products to market, and to assess how the target company could market and deliver future products for the betterment of the acquiring company.

Action Steps:

- Evaluate the additional strategic levers of product development: the capabilities of the target company to innovate and develop new products and intellectual property.

- Standardize corporate due diligence activities.

- Evaluate the key talent, including their capabilities and likelihood of remaining with the company.

3. Conduct Thorough Cultural Due Diligence

The expert panel stressed the importance of assessing the partners' cultural compatibility, defined as a fit of key facets of organizational culture that are critical to organizational success. For example, if one culture is very risk-averse and another is not, a problem will likely emerge if the combined organization is engaging in new product development.

Cultural compatibility and all of its ramifications need to be understood completely to ensure a successful M&A. The literature on M&A activity used familial metaphors to describe merger and acquisition, powerful language that further emphasized the significance of organizational members' experience as a result of a M&A. One internal M&A expert encouraged companies to be capable of articulating the key facets of cultural compatibility to the acquiring company. Identifying the "must haves" of cultural compatibility is like assessing marital compatibility; some compatibility issues are negotiable, while others could be considered "knockouts."

Executives who worked on a high-profile technology merger participated in cultural due diligence activities. They made the results from their culture surveys available as the selection process for executives of the combined firm began, and the survey results became a component of the selection process. They also introduced "fast-start" workshops to welcome the thousands of new employees to the acquiring company, and articulated the approach to working together.

Action Steps:

- Conduct extensive cultural due diligence surveys.

- Look at the cultural values of potential leaders being retained from the target company.

- Evaluate the underlying cultural factors and values that determine long-term success for the M&A.

- Determine the key facets of cultural compatibility important to your company.

4. Create a One-Year Post-Close Vision

M&A experts participating in this research said it was imperative that companies define what the combined company would look like one year after the M&A, including definitions of success for the overall organization, as well as its structure, financials, products, go-to-market, etc. They recommended developing a process for defining one-year success that involved acquiring executives to reach consensus. They also recommended naming a series of specific, bottom-line goals that needed to be achieved in the first 100 days—developed from the overall, first-year vision plan.

The goal of integration is to achieve key actions as quickly as possible—with "prudent," not reckless, speed. So, the experts advocated for integration planning and execution that could be done quickly. Establish very concrete objectives and timelines for creating synergy between the merging organizations, and set objective timelines for achieving objectives. Hold individuals personally responsible and accountable for meeting milestones and overall objectives.

These experts viewed a one-year post-close vision as critical to accomplishing M&A goals. One high-tech company took 60 executives off-line for five months within two weeks of the deal announcement, in order to integrate and develop the vision for the combined company.

Eventually, 2,000 employees were involved, demonstrating a successful balance between the need for confidentiality and the need for communication.

Action Steps:

- Establish 100-day bottom-line goals and focus corporate attention on completion.
- Develop a one-year post-merger vision.
- Plan, plan, plan.
- Plan relative to the scale of the M&A for the size of the company.
- Develop goals and track the progress against plans.

---

5. Conduct M&A Tracking and Integration Audits to Measure Performance

M&A activity requires detailed action plans, financial measures, financial tracking and reporting, clear decision making, and coordination across functions. Focus efforts on tracking the operational, financial, human resources, and strategic aspects of the combined firm, assessing what seems to be working well and determining areas that need improvement.

Establish M&A tracking and metrics in partnership with the business unit leader responsible for the target, once the acquisition is completed, because the business will own the metrics. Retention and product growth are two examples of the metrics tracked following an acquisition.

Action Steps:

- Track milestones for the integration until the goals of the M&A integration have been achieved.

- Select and monitor key metrics such as retention and product growth to evaluate the success of the M&A.

- Identify opportunities to capture and realize value to achieve organizational efficiencies.

6. Appoint an Accountable Integration Manager

The M&A experts also favor appointing an integration manager with primary responsibility and accountability for managing the integration process and acting as a bridge-builder between companies. Look for visible, internal candidates who are respected, available for this full-time role, and report to the business leader.

The experts regard hiring an integration manager as a M&A best practice. Internal M&A practitioners prefer the term "integration leader," and are less inclined to feel that the position needs to be full-time except for large M&As. In these professionals' view, while there may be critical moments in the process requiring the integration leader to work full time, most small M&As won't sustain such a period of intensity.

Action Steps:

- Evaluate the requirement for the integration manager to be full-time or part-time.

- Ensure the integration manager really knows the organization.

---

7. Use Transition Teams

M&A experts recommend assembling teams of employees from both parties to participate in integration planning. A launch meeting could clarify transition team charters, roles, and practices, and give cross-organizational teams the responsibility of overseeing integration planning and needs in different areas of the organization. Another recommendation: design the transition structure that will be used to integrate the two entities.

Transition teams (internal practitioners prefer the term "integration teams") that involve employees from both the target and the acquiring company ensure a successful deal completion. Consider the transition team a lever to share cultural intelligence between the two companies. My research indicates that the integration team should stay in place until 80% of the value capture intended for the acquisition is achieved. Value capture opportunities include reduced expenses from operating efficiencies achieved as a result of the M&A.

Action Steps:

- Select and implement the transition team.

- Put processes in place to escalate and enable fast decision making for these teams.

- Use transition teams to facilitate the sharing of culture.

8. Agree on Management Structure Early

Both internal and external M&A experts recommend that the new leadership team be named on Day One. If possible, appoint and announce other layers of the management structure at the same time. One expert commented that not announcing the leader on Day One is a "de-accelerator," but here's a caveat to that approach: Don't announce a new management structure in situations where the management team is going to be replaced.

Action Steps:

• Maintain M&A integration momentum by announcing the leadership on Day One.

9. Develop a Strategic Employee Communication Strategy

Both external and internal experts agree on the importance of developing and executing effective employee communications, particularly conveying how the transaction will impact organizational members. And secondly, get supervisors to talk to people one-on-one about their future after the change in control. Supervisors need to be aware of, and address, morale and personal issues individuals will face. Everyone in both organizations needs to understand the reasons for the combination.

Make communications open, honest, frequent, early, repeated, and strategic. Identify constituents, messages, mode, and frequency. Take all communication opportunities to drive the implementation of the strategy over time. Management and others should avoid using "killer phrases" such as "a merger of equals" (this does not exist) or "We will only tell employees something when there is something to tell." Information can always be shared... even if it is simply the progress of the deal or integration (Buono & Bowditch, 1989).

Communication is vital throughout the M&A process. The employee communication strategy is a clear opportunity to provide employees with information to reduce uncertainty.

Internal practitioners in particular emphasize the need for meetings with all employees, and a communication plan for customers, partners, investors, and the analyst community.

Action Steps:

- Communicate frequently with employees.
- Use a change model that helps move employees through the M&A change process.
- Extend the communication plan to include internal employees at both the acquiring and target companies.

5

Strengthening M&A Integration
The *5C Integration Model* ™

I developed the *5C Integration Model* ™ as a means of blending key findings from my review of the academic and business literature. It captures the best-practices recommendations from my panel of M&A experts while also reflecting my personal experience built over ten years in the fields of human resources and organization development.

The *5C Integration Model*™ serves as a guide for helping companies integrate, recall, and focus on the integration practices key to M&A success.

The *5C* themes are:

- Courtship
- Confidentiality
- Cultural Compatibility
- Communication
- Completion

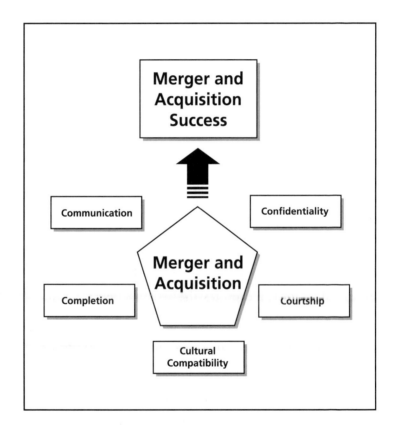

5C Theme #1: Courtship

The courtship theme articulates the importance of being clear about the reasons for the M&A, the strategy that the M&A activity supports, and the approach that will be taken, in entering into the relationship with the target company. Courtship is an approach to initiating the M&A relationship with a sense of clarity about expectations and strategy. Involvement in the development of the strategy shares knowledge within the company and creates a shared understanding of the strategy behind the M&A activity.

> *Many corporate M&A departments perceive their domain to be exclusively that of secretively finding target companies and signing the deals. In our experience, however, this dated approach does a tremendous disservice to the organization. The most effective M&A functions we have seen take a much more holistic approach, working with the [chief executive officer's] office and with people in organization development, HR, and the business units to map the entire M&A process, define specific roles and responsibilities, and manage the knowledge capturing process. The importance of accomplishing these tasks before the deal is started cannot be overemphasized.*
>
> —Galpin & Herndon

5C Theme #2: Confidentiality

The confidentiality theme emphasizes the importance of an M&A process that respects the need for confidentiality during its various stages.

Confidentiality, market sensitivities, and shareholder concerns allow an initial assessment to take place without full market scrutiny. M&A researchers Galpin and Herndon recommend that "counsel be obtained with respect to setting the appropriate time for integration planning to begin, and to establishing the deal-specific protocols that will govern the sharing of information and the coordination of activities." Additional measures, such as confidentiality agreements, can be introduced into the process to further respect business, regulatory, and market requirements.

5C Theme #3: Cultural Compatibility

Cultural compatibility as a theme can have significant impact on the ultimate success of M&A activity. A number of credible cultural assessment tools, such as culture surveys and facilitated focus groups, are available and should be utilized. As Dr. Edgar Schein points out, the challenge of assessing an organization's culture "is more a matter of surfacing assumptions, which will be recognizable once they have been uncovered." Identifying cultural compatibility on such core values as corporate ethics and quality is an important consideration in the assessment of the M&A. The impact of not assessing the degree of cultural similarity might have significant consequences for the combined firm, as cultural tensions and clashes between merging organizations are a common cause of combination related difficulties (Buono and Bowditch).

5C Theme #4: Communication

The communication theme emphasizes that an important aspect of M&A activity is frequent, honest, and candid communication.

Communication recognizes that the respect for confidentiality of the process and communication updates can be balanced in M&A activity, and that these two themes, if managed effectively, might lead to less uncertainty and insecurity for employees.

According to Buono and Bowditch, "organizational members are more likely to react positively when they are well informed—exposed to unfavorable as well as favorable possibilities—than when they are forced to rely on hearsay and speculation." One high tech company very active in M&As prioritizes communication to employees so that it always takes place immediately following deal closure.

The company recognizes that personal issues such as job security are uppermost in employees' minds in the initial days following an M&A announcement, and this practice ensures that employee concerns about job security and their role in the organization are dealt with first.

5C Theme #5: Completion

The completion theme focuses on the importance of completing the integration of the two companies. As a merger or acquisition nears completion, M&A deal finders focus on the next transaction while the business unit leaders, employees, and integration team members must focus on completing M&A activities in order to reach the identified goals.

As completion of the integration activity approaches, to leverage the M&A's full potential, address decisions about infrastructure, technology, people, and systems as part of this theme.

As Buono and Bowditch state, "attention to the details involved in a merger or acquisition requires a concern for both obvious and less apparent matters. Indeed, many of the 'little things' in an organizational combination signal the intention and concern of the acquiring firm."

The Interconnection of the 5Cs and M&A Best Practices

5Cs	Merger and Acquisition Best Practices
Courtship	Develop an overall goal and strategy that the merger and acquisition fits
Courtship and Confidentiality	Conduct thorough strategic, financial, and operational due diligence
Cultural Compatibility	Conduct thorough cultural due diligence
Completion and Confidentiality	Create a one-year post-close vision
Completion and Communication	Name an integration manager who is accountable for the success of the integration
Completion and Communication	Use transition teams
Completion	Conduct merger and acquisition tracking and integration audits to measure performance
Communication	Agree on management structure before the close of the deal
Communication	Develop an employee communication strategy

As shown in the diagram on page 55, the 5Cs are interconnected. They also relate in different ways to the Nine M&A Best Practices identified in my research, including the best practices' multiple themes.

For example, opportunities exist during an M&A to balance required levels of confidentiality with the need for general updates to employees on the merger activity.

An assessment of cultural compatibility relies heavily on communication and observation of the target company's culture.

Overall, of course, communication figures heavily throughout the entire M&A process as a best practice. It provides employees with valuable information and addresses the uncertainty that exists during this period of transition.

Conclusion

M&A practitioners have rich opportunities to humanize what is often treated by companies as merely a business and financial transaction. Focusing on the human dimension of M&A will significantly impact the bottom-line success, result in less organizational turmoil, and ultimately determine the overall success of M&A transactions.

View M&A as an activity good for both the organization and employees rather than as a time of employee uncertainty and insecurity.

Organization development practitioners have significant opportunities to play a key role in M&A activities, which can be viewed as a large, complex change management project. They have the tools and resources to provide recommendations, processes, and interventions necessary for the successful navigation of all kinds of change management projects, including M&A activity. Their early involvement in the due diligence process might contribute to more successful integrations between two corporate cultures. By assisting with cultural due diligence through employee interventions, they can also strengthen and accelerate the integration process.

To have a *Done Deal*, attend to the best practices and use the *5C Integration Model*™ as a guide for strengthening your organization's mergers and acquisitions.

Part II

5C Self-Assessment Workbook

5C Theme #1: Courtship

Courtship is an approach to initiating the M&A with a sense of clarity about expectations and strategy.

Defining the Overall Strategy and Goal

Is the proposed M&A consistent with your business strategy?

Yes, because ...

No, but it will be if...

Consider why this deal is being pursued. Can you cite specific reasons/rationale for how this transaction will positively impact your business?

1.

2.

3.

4.

5.

Notes:

5C Theme #2: Confidentiality

Confidentiality, market sensitivities,
and shareholder concerns allow an initial assessment
to take place without full market scrutiny.

What are the key strategic levers associated with the M&A?

1. Human Resources Capabilities:

2. Sales & Marketing Strengths:

3. Supplier Networks:

4. Cultural Orientations:

5. New Product Development Capabilities:

6. Potential for Intellectual Property Creation:

7. Customers

8. Others:

Notes:

Key Talent Assessment

1. Who are the key players who must be retained after this transaction is completed?

2. How critical is each individual to achieving the expected outcomes of the M&A?

3. What is the likelihood of each player to remain?

4. What retention strategies and mechanisms will you deploy to ensure retention?

Name	Role	Criticality	Retention Likelihood	Retention Strategy

5C Theme #3: Cultural Compatibility

Identifying cultural compatibility on core values is an important consideration in the assessment of the M&A.

Cultural Due Diligence

1. What are the cultural values of the new organization's top leaders?

Name	Values

2. What are the underlying cultural factors for the acquiring company?

3. What are the underlying cultural factors for the target company?

4. Where are the complements between the cultures?

5. Where are the potential conflicts between the cultures?

6. Which aspects of the acquiring company's culture do you wish to retain?

7. Which aspects of the target company's culture do you wish to retain?

8. Which aspects of the acquiring company's culture do you wish to evolve or discard?

9. Which aspects of the target company's culture do you wish to evolve or discard?

Notes:

5C Theme #4: Communication

*The communication theme emphasizes
that an important aspect of M&A activity is
frequent, honest, and candid communication.*

Clarifying Leadership Structure

1. Have the key leadership team members been identified?

2. Will the organization be ready to announce the management structure and key players on Day One, post-close?

3. Who is responsible for developing the announcement?

4. Who is responsible for deploying the announcement?

Developing a Strategic Employee Communication Strategy

1. Have messages been prepared to communicate to employees how the M&A transaction will impact them?

2. Have schedules been developed to regularly communicate updates to employees at both companies regarding the M&A transaction's status? Are these schedules synchronized so everyone is receiving information in the same time frame?

3. When will supervisors/managers be briefed and equipped with the materials that will enable them to communicate and address employees' questions?

4. Who is responsible for developing the employee communications strategy?

5. Who is responsible for developing the communications materials?

6. Who is responsible for leading the communications effort at the acquiring company?

7. Who is responsible for leading the communications effort at the target company?

8. Are the key messages consistent between the acquiring and target companies?

5C Theme #5: Completion

The completion theme focuses on the importance of completing the integration of the two companies.

Creating a One-Year Post-Close Vision

1. What will it take for you to consider this transaction "complete"?

2. What will it take for the organization to consider this transaction "successful"?

3. Using the above two as a definition for a successful transaction, what are key 100-day bottom-line goals?

4. Which performance metrics will be most important for tracking progress?

5. Is there consensus among the M&A team for a definition of "success"?

Integration Management

1. Who is the single individual who has the ultimate accountability for the M&A integration?

2. Does the integration leader have the appropriate authority, as well as the responsibility, for leading this effort?

3. In the organization, whose participation will be critical for this transaction to be a success?

4. Who might be "shadow influencers" or informal leaders whose participation (or lack thereof) could influence this transaction's outcome?

5. Who should be assigned to the transition team? Who among this team has responsibility for helping share or shape the organization's new culture?

Tracking and Integration Metrics

1. What are the key performance metrics that must be monitored to ensure the integration is proceeding as expected?

2. What are key milestones for each metric? (Note: these may be operational, financial, HR-related, and/or strategic in nature.)

Metric	Key Milestones

About the Research

The research was completed as a thesis project within the Master of Science in Organization Development program at Pepperdine University.

M&A researchers and practitioners who had published on the subject of M&A and had several years experience in the field were included in the expert panel.

The Delphi Methodology was used with the expert panel to achieve consensus using a broad range of input from respected contributors to the field of mergers and acquisitions. Internal M&A practitioners were interviewed at Best Practice companies for their views on the M&A Best Practices identified by the Delphi expert panel.

The expert panel included:

Ron N. Ashkenas, Robert H. Schaffer & Associates, *Integration managers: Special leaders for special times.* Harvard Business Review. (2000)

Anthony F. Buono, Management and Sociology, Bentley College, *SEAM-less post merger integration strategies: A cause for concern.* Journal of Organizational Change Management. (2003)

Richard M. DiGeorgio, Richard M. DiGeorgio & Associates, *Making Mergers and Acquisitions Work: What we know and don't know.* (2002)

Timothy J. Galpin, Graduate School of Management, University of Dallas, *The Complete Guide to Mergers and Acquisitions: Process Tools to Support M&A Integration*. San Francisco: Jossey-Bass. (2000)

David B. Jemison, McCombs School of Business, University of Texas at Austin, *Managing Acquisitions*. (1991)

Jeffrey A. Krug, Walker College of Business, Appalachian State University, *Why do they keep leaving?* Harvard Business Review. (2003)

Mitchell Lee Marks, Department of Management, San Francisco State University, *Joining Forces: Making One Plus One Equal Three in Mergers, Acquisitions, and Alliances*. (1998)

Nick J. Mastracchio Jr., School of Business, State University of New York, *Differences between mergers and acquisitions*. Journal of Accountancy. (2002)

Many of the members of the expert panel have several publications in addition to the one cited above. Please see the bibliography for the complete citation, including co-authors.

Bibliography

Ashkenas, R. N., & Francis, S. C. (2000). Integration Managers: Special Leaders for Special Times. *Harvard Business Review, 78*(6), 108–119.

Ashkenas, R. N., DeMonaco, L. J., & Francis, S. C. (1998). Making the Deal Real: How GE Capital Integrates Acquisitions. *Harvard Business Review, 76*(1), 165–177.

Bunnell, D., & Brate, A. (Eds.). (2000). *Making the Cisco Connection: The Story Behind the Real Internet Superpower.* New York: John Wiley and Sons.

Buono, A. F. (2003). SEAM-less Post-Merger Integration Strategies: A Cause for Concern. *Journal of Organizational Change Management, 16*(1), 90–98.

Buono, A. F., & Nurick, A. J. (1992). Intervening in the Middle: Coping Strategies in Mergers and Acquisitions. *Human Resource Planning, 15*(2), 19–33.

Buono, A. F., & Bowditch, J. L. (1989). *The Human Side of Mergers and Acquisitions: Managing Collisions Between People, Cultures, and Organizations.* San Francisco: Jossey-Bass.

Cartwright, S., & Cooper, G. L. (1996). *Managing Mergers, Acquisitions and Strategic Alliances: Integrating People and Cultures* (2nd ed.). Oxford, United Kingdom: Butterworth-Heinemann.

Clark, P. J. (1991). *Beyond the Deal: Optimizing Merger and Acquisition Value.* New York: Harper Collins.

Collins, J. (2001). *Good to Great: Why Some Companies Make the Leap . . . and Others Don't.* New York: Harper Collins.

Couger, J. D. (1988). Key Human Resources Issues in IS in the 1990s: Views of IS Executives Versus Human Resource Executives. *Information and Management, 14*(4), 161–174.

Croyle, R., & Kager, P. (2002). Giving Mergers a Head Start. *Harvard Business Review, 80*(10), 20–21.

Cummings, T. G., & Worley, C. G. (2001). *Organization Development and Change* (7th ed.). Cincinnati, OH: South-Western.

Dalkey, N., & Helmer, O. (1963). An Experimental Application of the Delphi Method to the Use of Experts. *Management Science, 9*(3), 458–468.

DeMan, D. (2002). Know When to Bail. *Pharmaceutical Executive, 22*(11), 102–108.

Denison, D. R. (1990). *Corporate Culture and Organizational Effectiveness.* New York: John Wiley and Sons.

DiGeorgio, R. (2002). Making Mergers and Acquisitions Work: What We Know and Don't Know—Part 1. *Journal of Change Management, 3*(2), 134–149.

Dillavou, J. (2002). The Three Questions to Ask Before Buying a Business. *International Tax Review, 13*(10), 16–18.

Eccles, R. G., Lanes, K. L., & Wilson, T. C. (1999). Are You Paying Too Much for That Acquisition? *Harvard Business Review, 77*(4), 136–147.

Fusfeld, A. R., & Foster, R. N. (1971). The Delphi Technique: Survey and Comment. *Business Horizons, 14*(3), 63–75.

Galpin, T. J., & Herndon, M. (2000). *The Complete Guide to Mergers and Acquisitions: Process Tools to Support M&A Integration.* San Francisco: Jossey-Bass.

Haspeslagh, P. C., & Jemison, D. B. (1991). *Managing Acquisitions.* New York: Free Press.

Kotter, J. P. (1995, March-April). Leading Change: Why Transformation Efforts Fail. *Harvard Business Review, 73*(2), 59–67.

Kotter, J. P. (1996). *Leading Change.* Boston: Harvard Business School Press.

Krug, J. A. (2003). Why Do They Keep Leaving? *Harvard Business Review, 81*(2), 14–15.

Love, P., & Gibson, S. (1999). Hidden Sore Points That Can Thwart a Culture Match. *Mergers and Acquisitions, 33*(6), 51–56.

Marks, M. L. (1999). Adding Cultural Fit to Your Diligence Checklist. *Mergers and Acquisitions, 34*(3), 14–20.

Marks, M. L., & Mirvis, P. H. (1998). *Joining Forces: Making One Plus One Equal Three in Mergers, Acquisitions, and Alliances.* San Francisco: Jossey-Bass.

Marquess, K. (2003). The Clean Room. *ABA Journal, 89*(2), 82.

Mastracchio, Jr., N. J., & Zunitch, V. M. (2002). Differences Between Mergers and Acquisitions. *Journal of Accountancy, 194*(5), 38–41.

Mirvis, P. H., & Marks, M. L. (1992). The Human Side of Merger Planning: Assessing and Analyzing. *Human Resource Planning, 15*(3), 69–92.

Mitchell, V. M. (1991). The Delphi Technique: An Exposition and Application. *Technology Analysis & Strategic Management, 3*(4), 333–358.

Pfeffer, J., & Tromley C. I. (1995, February). Producing Sustainable Competitive Advantage Through the Effective Management of People. *Academy of Management Executive, 9*(1), 55–73.

Rappaport, A. (1998). Calculating the Value-Creation Potential of a Deal. *Mergers and Acquisitions, 33*(1), 33–44.

Robb, D. (2003). Winning Their Hearts, Their Minds and Their Databases: Following an Acquisition, Merging Company Cultures and Integrating Business Systems are the Most Vital Challenges. *Information Strategy, 19*(3), 12–17.

Rovit, S., & Lemire, C. (2003). Your Best M&A Strategy. *Harvard Business Review, 81*(3), 16–17.

Schein, E. H. (1984). Coming to a New Awareness of Organizational Culture. *Sloan Management Review, 25*(2), 3–16.

Schein, E. H. (1997). *Organization Culture and Leadership* (2nd ed.). San Francisco: Jossey-Bass.

Sirower, M. L. (1998a, January-February). Imagined Synergy: A Prescription for a No-Win Deal. *Mergers and Acquisitions, 32*(4), 23–29.

Sirower, M. L. (1998b, May-June). Constructing a Synergistic Base for Premier Deals. *Mergers and Acquisitions, 32*(6), 42–49.

Tersine, R. J., & Riggs, W. E. (1976). The Delphi Technique: A Long Range Planning Tool. *Business Horizons, 19*(2), 51–57.

Tetenbaum, T. J. (1999). Seven Key Practices That Improve the Chance for Expected Integration and Synergies. *Organizational Dynamics, 28*(2), 22–36.

Van de Ven, A. H., & Delbecq, A. L. (1974). The Effectiveness of Nominal, Delphi, and Interacting Group Decision-Making Processes. *Academy of Management Journal, 17*(4), 605–622.

Vinten, G. (1993). Employee Relations in Mergers and Acquisitions. *Employee Relations, 15*(4), 47–65.

Learn More about Change Management

For more information about Change Management and Beth Page's speaking, coaching and consulting services, go to the website at *www.dreamcatcher-consulting.com*.

For Change Management Resources

Visit *www.dreamcatcher-consulting.com* to subscribe to *Dreamcatchers*, a monthly change management newsletter with tools, tips, book recommendations and exercises.

Buy the Book

You may purchase *Done Deal* through the internet at *www.authenticitypress.com*. Discounts are available for volume purchases.

Your Comments

Feel free to email Beth your comments about this book. She can be contacted at *beth@dreamcatcher-consulting.com*.

Websites for more information:

www.dreamcatcher-consulting.com
www.authenticitypress.com
www.mbethpage.com

Order More Books

Email orders: *orders@authenticitypress.com*

By mail: Authenticity Press
          Suite 554, 185-911 Yates Street
          Victoria, BC, V8V 4Y9

By Phone: 250-483-6729

Yes, I want ____ copies of *Done Deal: Your Guide to Merger and Acquisition Integration* at $21.95 CDN each plus $5.00 S&H plus 7% GST within Canada.
Please email or call to ask about international shipping rates.
Discounts for volume purchases.

Name _____

Address_____

City _____

Province/State _____

Postal Code/Zip Code _____

Country _____

Telephone _____

Email _____
        (used for billing purposes only)

Please enclose check or money order payable to
Authenticity Press
Or visit *www.authenticitypress.com*